This book belongs to

. . . .

To Adelina, Jeremiah, Solomon, Eli Crew, and Ainsley,

Every day with you is my favorite.

To Phil, I could never ask for a better friend.

You are our world.

To Eileen, for making the work of mothering so beautiful.

You are never forgotten.

And to Dad for everything from front yard apple pie

to Nightingale Hall to this very moment.

Marshmallows and Toast
Text copyright © 2025 by Jessica Vana
Illustration copyright © 2025 by Mandy Sutcliffe
All rights reserved.

Published in the United States of America by Credo House Publishers
a division of Credo Communications, LLC, Grand Rapids, MI
credohousepublishers.com

Unless otherwise noted, Scripture quotations are from the Holy Bible, New International Version®,
NIV® Copyright ©1973, 1978, 1984, 2011 by Biblica, Inc.®
Used by permission. All rights reserved worldwide.

ISBN: 978-1-62586-317-1

Illustrations by Mandy Sutcliffe
Interior design and typesetting by Sharon VanLoozenoord
Editing by Crystal Bowman

Printed in the United States of America

First edition

We were sitting on the porch swing, our legs dangling in the fading sunlight, when the children dared to ask their favorite question.
"Mom, how much do you love us?"

Well now, let's see . . .

I love you more than cuppy cakes
on a Friday afternoon.

I love you more than a bright bouquet
of freshly stringed balloons.

I love you more than a floppy dog
at the bottom of the bed.

I love you more than when you could go play
but cook with me instead.

I love you more than tiny toes in frothy waves on sandy shores.

I love you more than window shopping
  at all our favorite stores.

I love you more than birthday brownies from our own cozy kitchen.

I love you more than the daily things you have made me vastly rich in.

I love you more than riding bikes
downtown in the month of May,

More than boardgames

and epic fort-builds
   on a rainy holiday.

I love you more than summer popsicles, reading books on our back deck.

I love you more than Sunday naps, your arms around my neck.

I love you more than inside jokes from stories that we've shared.

I love you more than road trips and all the hikes we've ever dared.

I love you more than puffy covers and crispy cool bed sheets.
I love you more than all the messy piles of books we love to read.

I love you more than treasures
we've collected through the years.

I love you more than when our laughing
turns into laughing tears.

I love you more than tea parties with our stuffies and our friends,

 More than the times you could stay mad

but decide to make amends.

I love you more than sandaled feet on sunkissed golden skin.

I love you more than salty mist and crispy ocean wind.

I love you more than that first cold drink from Grandma's garden hose,

More than the way you make me snort-laugh my coffee through my nose.

I love you more than stretching in cool grass right at dawn.

I love the way you look like a tiger-cub, but only when you yawn.

I love you more than spicy cocoa on a quiet winter night.
I love you more than the scarf you made that fits my neck just right.

I love you more than tent-camping with onward gazing stars.

I love you more than catching July fireflies in jars.

I love you more than all the moments I try to freeze the most.

I love you more than all the things I'll ever have or do.
I love you more and most and much, all the way to Timbuktu.

So if you're lonely, lost, or scared or wondering if someone truly cares,
I always have. I always will. And I completely do.